OPENING THE ROAD

Victor Hugo Green and His Green Book

by **Keila V. Dawson**

illustrated by **Alleanna Harris**

beaming books
MINNEAPOLIS

Victor Hugo Green was tired of hearing no.

Victor loved the freedom of driving on the open road, but too often the road was closed to him. It was like this for most Black people in the United States.

When he and his wife, Alma, traveled from New York to Virginia to visit family, they risked getting turned away, yelled at, even hurt.

Black motorists were told:

No food . . .

No vacancy . . .

No bathroom . . .

for Black people.

White American travelers could stop at any
roadside restaurant, hotel, or restroom.

But Black Americans had to pack cold food, blankets,
and pillows for sleeping in the car . . . and a make-do toilet.

In southern states, Jim Crow laws kept
Black and white Americans apart.
No drinking from the same water fountain.

No walking through the same door.

No sitting together.

And the separate Black spaces were always
second-class, if they existed at all.

On road trips, with nowhere safe to stop and stay,
Black motorists often drove at night—all night.
If they had an accident, ambulances and
hospitals refused to help them. If they were lucky,
they could find a Black funeral director to bring
them to a hospital. But there wasn't always
a hospital nearby that treated Black patients.

Up north and out west, Black drivers feared
getting lost or having car trouble in the wrong town at
the wrong time. At sunset in "sundown towns,"
the sound of a siren or a white man's wave signaled:
Leave now.

Even in Victor's home state of New York, where there were antidiscrimination laws, many restaurants, businesses, schools, and parks did not welcome Black people.

One day, Victor read a Jewish newspaper with information about Jewish-owned hotels and vacation resorts in New York. He discovered a guide for Jewish people with lists of stores that sold kosher food. In the 1930s, Jewish Americans couldn't go everywhere they wanted to either.

This gave Victor an idea. What if he wrote a book with information about where Black Americans were safe and welcome?

So Victor asked his friends and neighbors in Harlem where they safely dined, shopped, and played in the city. Victor worked as a mail carrier. Along his postal route, Victor asked folks about places that were welcoming to Black people too.

After lugging his heavy mail sack in heat, rain, sleet, or snow all day, Victor worked on the book at night. Sometimes he'd nod off while sorting and compiling his growing lists.

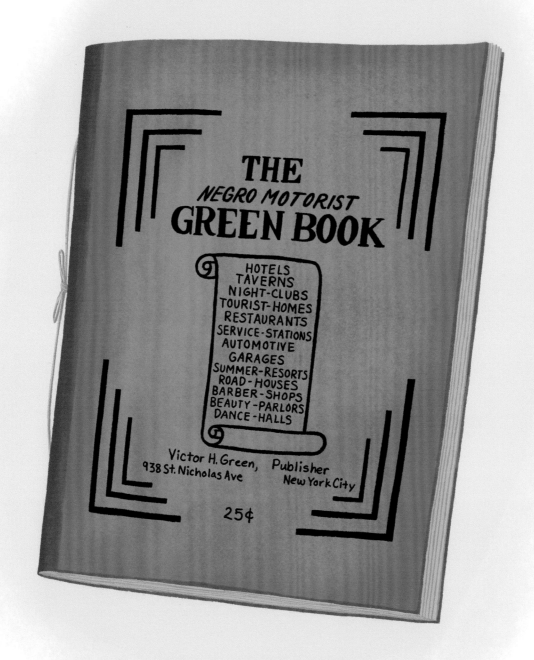

Victor finished *The Negro Motorist Green Book* in 1936. It was a ten-page guide filled with safe spaces and friendly faces for Black travelers in New York City. The following year, he updated the guide. "Let's all get together and make motoring better," he wrote.

With copies in hand, Victor visited Black churches and social clubs to persuade New Yorkers to buy his book.

It sold like hotcakes!

Customers called it the Green Book and begged Victor to include other states in his guide.

So Victor wrote letters asking mail carriers all over the country for the names and addresses of places that welcomed Black customers.

Replies poured in. Victor and Alma worked together to expand the guide. Two years later, the Green Book more than doubled in size to twenty-eight pages.

With Victor's Green Book, Black travelers knew where to go and who to trust.

Hungry? Check the Green Book.

Tired? Check the Green Book.

Sick? Check the Green Book.

To keep the guide current, Victor asked readers for recommendations. He hired sales agents to find Black-owned businesses to add.

News about the guide mostly spread by word of mouth. Then in 1940, Victor happily announced that the US government named it an "official Negro travel guide." When a national chain of gas stations started selling the Green Book, travelers filling their tanks were happy to find the helpful guide. The Green Book flew off the shelves!

In cities with no hotels willing to rent to Black people, some Black female entrepreneurs rented out rooms in their homes.

Tourists showed up at all hours of the day—or night—
on strangers' doorsteps. But with the Green Book,
they knew they were arriving somewhere safe.

"Carry your Green Book with you,"
Victor urged. "You may need it."

The Green Book became more than a travel guide. It also helped readers learn about Black achievements and Black history. The guide steered families toward cities with thriving Black communities. It listed colleges that accepted Black students.

Even famous Black singers, musicians, movie stars, and athletes used the Green Book.

More than two million copies of the Green Book were sold. It made it possible for Black families to enjoy vacations. They went hiking in the mountains, swimming on the seashore, and horseback riding in the countryside at businesses run by Black owners.

In the 1950s and '60s, Black Americans were also marching, staging sit-ins, and sitting with white allies on segregated buses and at restaurants.

They were building a civil rights movement
to protest racial inequality.

Victor dreamed of a day when Black citizens wouldn't need the Green Book at all, "when we as a race will have equal opportunities and privileges in the United States."

When some states stopped separating Black and white travelers on trains, on buses, and in airports, fewer copies of the Green Book sold.

In 1964, the United States Congress passed a law that made separating people by race illegal.

The 1966–67 Green Book was the last edition published.

The fight against racism still had—
and still has—a long way to go.

But now there was . . .

no legal segregation . . .

no legal discrimination . . .

no Green Book for Black people.

Just like Victor dreamed.

Sadly, Victor Hugo Green himself never got to eat in just any restaurant, sleep in any hotel, or use any restroom he wanted. Victor died in 1960. For years afterward, his wife and business partner, Alma, made sure the Green Book remained in print.

Victor was just four years old in 1896 when the US Supreme Court decision in *Plessy v. Ferguson* upheld the "separate but equal" state laws. These laws kept white citizens and Black citizens segregated and limited the places where Black Americans were allowed. They were restricted to living in segregated neighborhoods, couldn't use public buildings or services designated for "whites only," and were less likely to get jobs that paid well. Laws in southern states were very strict. When northern states passed laws to protect Black Americans, the social practice of discrimination still continued.

The Green Book wasn't the first or only guide for Black travelers, but it was the most successful. As a mail carrier, Victor Hugo Green had access to over two thousand other Black postal workers across the country. This network provided him with information and helped spread the word about his book. It became an international travel guide as well, offering listings in Canada, Bermuda, and Mexico. Victor Green even organized tours, made reservations, and arranged cruises to Africa, South America, Europe, and more. The only time Green didn't publish his annual guide was during World War II, from 1942 to 1945.

Today, traveling is easier, but it still isn't always safe for Black drivers. In the state of Ohio, an unarmed Black man, Samuel DuBose, lost his life in 2015 at the hands of a University of Cincinnati police officer at a traffic stop because his car did not have a front license plate. In 2016, Philando Castile died at the hands of a Minnesota police officer when stopped because the officer said he looked like a robbery suspect. There is justified fear among Black Americans when on the road. And unfair treatment of Black citizens reaches beyond traffic stops. Today, organized protests and demonstrations against injustice in policing have grown into the civil rights campaign known as Black Lives Matter.

Black Americans are creating new versions of the Green Book for Black travelers. For example, Martinique Lewis created the ABC Travel Green Book series, a collection of travel guides featuring Black-owned tours, restaurants, and places of interest to Black locals around the world. And Crystal Egli and Parker McMullen Bushman are working to develop a Digital Green Book website that lists businesses, parks, restaurants, stores, and towns that Black people can feel safe traveling to.

Even as movements build and some things improve, racist systems and practices persist. We must continue to work together to stop discrimination by getting to know people who are different from us, practicing being a good neighbor, and speaking up when we see injustice.

1892 Victor Hugo Green is born in New York.

1925 Henry Ford's assembly-line production lowers the cost of the Model T, allowing more Americans to own a motor car.

1921 The Federal Aid Highway Act passes in Congress to fund a national highway system, increasing travel and tourism.

1934 Standard Oil Company of New Jersey hires a Black American, James A. Jackson, to help promote the company in the Black community.

1954 The Supreme Court decision in *Brown v. Board of Education* determines that school segregation is unconstitutional.

1947 Victor Green and James A. Jackson of Standard Oil Company of New Jersey sign a contract to sell the Green Book at its Esso Gas Stations.

1957 The US Congress authorizes a Civil Rights Commission to investigate complaints about states that do not allow Black Americans their civil right to vote.

1961 The Interstate Commerce Commission prohibits segregation in any transportation-terminal facilities and forbids the posting of signs separating people by race.

1960 Victor Green dies in New York at age 67. His wife, Alma, continues to publish the Green Book.

1962 Businessman Langley Waller and editorial cartoonist Melvin Tapley buy publishing rights to the Green Book.

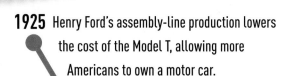

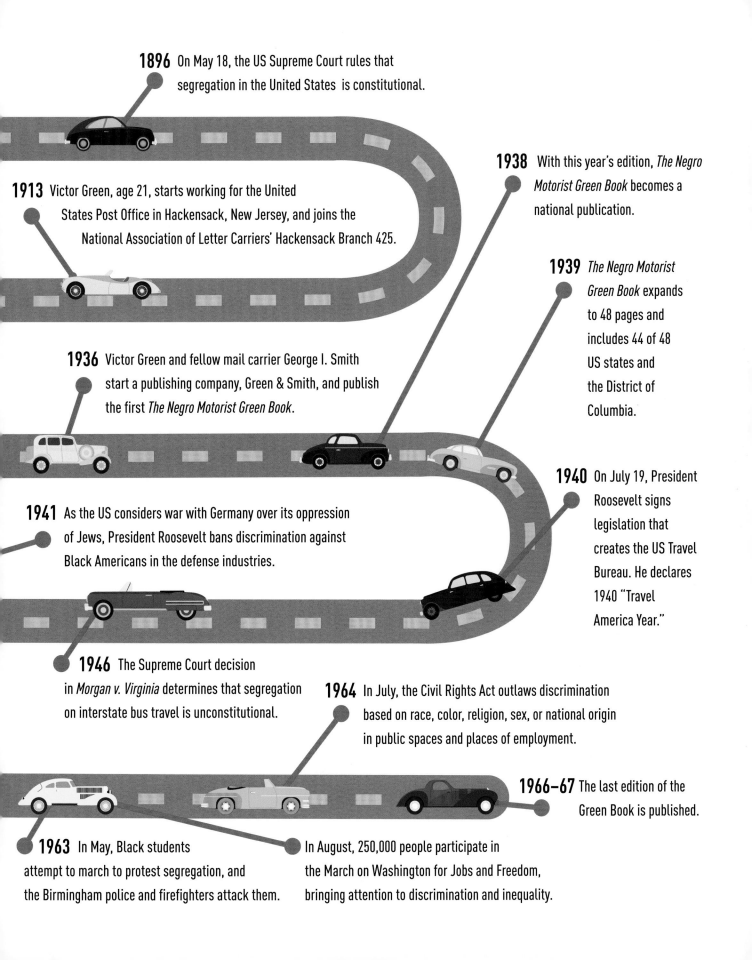

1896 On May 18, the US Supreme Court rules that segregation in the United States is constitutional.

1913 Victor Green, age 21, starts working for the United States Post Office in Hackensack, New Jersey, and joins the National Association of Letter Carriers' Hackensack Branch 425.

1938 With this year's edition, *The Negro Motorist Green Book* becomes a national publication.

1939 *The Negro Motorist Green Book* expands to 48 pages and includes 44 of 48 US states and the District of Columbia.

1936 Victor Green and fellow mail carrier George I. Smith start a publishing company, Green & Smith, and publish the first *The Negro Motorist Green Book*.

1941 As the US considers war with Germany over its oppression of Jews, President Roosevelt bans discrimination against Black Americans in the defense industries.

1940 On July 19, President Roosevelt signs legislation that creates the US Travel Bureau. He declares 1940 "Travel America Year."

1946 The Supreme Court decision in *Morgan v. Virginia* determines that segregation on interstate bus travel is unconstitutional.

1964 In July, the Civil Rights Act outlaws discrimination based on race, color, religion, sex, or national origin in public spaces and places of employment.

1966–67 The last edition of the Green Book is published.

1963 In May, Black students attempt to march to protest segregation, and the Birmingham police and firefighters attack them.

In August, 250,000 people participate in the March on Washington for Jobs and Freedom, bringing attention to discrimination and inequality.

Selected Bibliography

Loewen, James W. *Sundown Towns: A Hidden Dimension of American Racism.* New York: Simon & Schuster, 2006.

"Navigating the Green Book." NYPL Labs. http://publicdomain.nypl.org/green-book-map/.

Rubio, Philip F. *There's Always Work at the Post Office: African American Postal Workers and the Fight for Jobs, Justice, and Equality.* Chapel Hill: University of North Carolina Press, 2010.

Schomburg Center for Research in Black Culture, Jean Blackwell Hutson Research and Reference Division, The New York Public Library. "Green Book Collection: 1936–64 *The New York Public Library Digital Collections.* 1936–64. https://digitalcollections.nypl.org/collections/the-green-book.

Sorin, Gretchen Sullivan. *Driving While Black: African American Travel and the Road to Civil Rights.* Liveright Publishing Corporation, 2020.

Sugrue, Thomas J. *Sweet Land of Liberty: The Forgotten Struggle for Civil Rights in the North* New York: Random House, 2008. Kindle Edition.

Taylor, Candacy A. *Overground Railroad: The Green Book and the Roots of Black Travel in America.* New York: Abrams Press, 2020.

Quotations

"Let's all get together and make motoring better."

—Victor H. Green, *The Negro Motorist Green Book*, 1937 edition

"Carry your Green Book with you. You may need it."

—Victor H. Green, *The Negro Motorist Green Book*, 1946 edition

". . . when we as a race will have equal opportunities and privileges in the United States."

—Victor H. Green, *The Negro Motorist Green Book*, 1948 edition

Published in 2021 by Beaming Books, an imprint of 1517 Media. All rights reserved.
No part of this book may be reproduced without the written permission of the publisher.
Email copyright@1517.media. Printed in Canada.

27 26 25 24 23 22 21   1 2 3 4 5 6 7 8

Hardcover ISBN: 978-1-5064-6791-7
Ebook ISBN: 978-1-5064-6892-1

Library of Congress Cataloging-in-Publication Data

Names: Dawson, Keila V., author. | Harris, Alleanna, illustrator.
Title: Opening the road : Victor Hugo Green and his Green Book / by Keila
    V. Dawson ; illustrated by Alleanna Harris.
Other titles: Victor Hugo Green and his Green Book
Description: [Minneapolis, Minnesota] : [Beaming Books], [2021] | Includes
    bibliographical references. | Audience: Ages 3-8 | Summary: "A
    nonfiction picture book about The Green Book, a travel guide for African
    Americans during segregation, and the man who wrote it"-- Provided by
    publisher.
Identifiers: LCCN 2020029836 (print) | LCCN 2020029837 (ebook) | ISBN
    9781506467917 (hardcover) | ISBN 9781506468921 (ebook)
Subjects: LCSH: Green, Victor H.--Juvenile literature. | African
    Americans--Travel--History--20th century--Juvenile literature. | African
    American automobile drivers--History--20th century--Juvenile literature.
    | Automobile travel--United States--History--20th century--Juvenile
    literature. | Segregation in transportation--United
    States--History--20th century--Juvenile literature. | African
    Americans--Segregation--History--20th century--Juvenile literature. |
    African Americans--Social conditions--20th century--Juvenile literature.
    | African American authors--Biography--Juvenile literature. | Travel
    writers--Biography--Juvenile literature.
Classification: LCC E185.61 .D385 2021 (print) | LCC E185.61 (ebook) |
    DDC 305.896/0730904--dc23
LC record available at https://lccn.loc.gov/2020029836
LC ebook record available at https://lccn.loc.gov/2020029837

65087; 9781506467917; NOV2020

Beaming Books
510 Marquette Avenue
Minneapolis, MN 55402
Beamingbooks.com